INTERACTIVE **WORKBOOK**

PATHWAY
TO HEALING

A Guide for Adult Survivors of Childhood Sexual Abuse

Thank you to Carolyn Forchè for your contribution to *Pathway to Healing*.

BOOKLOGIX
Alpharetta, GA

The resources contained within this book are provided for informational purposes only and should not be used to replace the specialized training and professional judgment of a healthcare or mental healthcare professional. Angela's Voice and the publisher of this work cannot be held responsible for the use of the information provided. Always consult a licensed mental health professional before making any decision regarding treatment of yourself or others.

Copyright © 2011, 2023 by Angela's Voice

Second Edition

All rights reserved. No part of this book may be reproduced or transmitted in any form or by any means, electronic or mechanical, including photocopying, recording, or any information storage and retrieval system, without permission in writing from the author.

ISBN: 978-1-61005-985-5

This ISBN is the property of BookLogix for the express purpose of sales and distribution of this title. The content of this book is the property of the copyright holder only. BookLogix does not hold any ownership of the content of this book and is not liable in any way for the materials contained within. The views and opinions expressed in this book are the property of the Author/Copyright holder, and do not necessarily reflect those of BookLogix.

∞ This paper meets the requirements of ANSI/NISO Z39.48-1992 (Permanence of Paper)

Workbook text and editing by Carolyn Forchè, Angela Williams.
Design and Illustration by Mark Sandlin. Design production by Felicia Kahn.

042023

DEDICATION

This workbook is dedicated to you who will take the first step toward healing from the ravages of childhood sexual abuse you've suffered. Child sexual abuse proves that, indeed, bad things do happen to good people. As men and women who've been where you are, we have released our emotional baggage and the pain of the past one voice at a time. We have broken the power of being threatened into silence that kept us hostage. As we dedicate this **Pathway to Healing** workbook to you and you embark on the exciting venture of sharing your voice with others through this process, we invite you to do as we have done while beginning our journey. We urge you to read **From Sorrows to Sapphires** and **Loving Me: After Abuse** by Angela Williams. Not only will you experience Angela's journey from abuse to healing, but you can jumpstart your walk into freedom. Her story and transparency has impacted many survivors.

Unfortunate as those long years were for her, the experiences she gained through a nightmare of sorrows have taught her the principles, values, attributes, and rigors of reliance upon God to bring wholeness and healing to her life. She has been set free from the bondage of mental and emotional paralysis that tormented her for years. She offers that same deliverance to you, through the power of God, and for that reason, this work is dedicated to you. It is your time to heal.

CONTENTS

Introduction 1

LESSON I: You are not alone 5

LESSON II: The power of two: don't start the path alone 8

LESSON III: It is time to break the silence 11

LESSON IV: Keys to breaking the silence 16

LESSON V: The purging power of prayer 20

LESSON VI: Unmasking 24

LESSON VII: Break old habits and self-destructive patterns 26

LESSON VIII: Facing foe(s) by confronting in love 30

LESSON IX: Forgiveness: the final answer to true healing 34

LESSON X: Outreach & support: the healing that keeps on healing 40

LESSON XI: Celebrating the vitality of victory 43

Angela's Voice 45

Join the Angela's Voice Movement 47

INTRODUCTION

The Need for Healing & Why It Is a *Spiritual* Need

Finally, and not a moment too soon, the conscience of America is slowly responding to a demanding social subpoena to heed the problem of sexual abuse. While there are movements and organizations established to confront this malady head on, they often deal, thankfully so, with preventing continued abuse, or providing help and counseling for sexually abused *children*. This is still a major work in progress, because the help children receive usually comes when those children have been bold enough to speak out, or when their abuse has been directly reported to authorities by an intervening adult. But what of the wounded child *still* living in millions of adults crying out for help or deliverance?

More often than not that cry is a silent one, causing a life of misery for men and women who have never dealt with the trauma that childhood sexual abuse has caused. And, more often than not, their unhealed trauma is attributed to a social stigma that teaches by its silence that these problems are not to be talked about. That protected silence is the very bane – the wretched undoing of society's responsibility to confront this crime against the human body, soul and spirit. Again, thankfully, there is a move to reach out and respond to the adult survivor whose soul is crying out for help, a cry to be free of the torment experienced almost daily. Angela's Voice is such a movement. Its mission is to do what its name declares: To give VOICE to the silence that has imprisoned men and women.

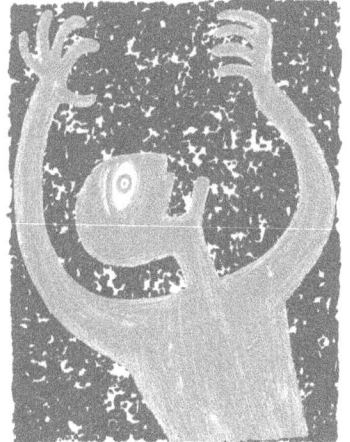

Now, with Angela's Voice's support systems, survivors can discover how they can peel away the painful layers of the past. Men and women are free to face the issues that have held them captive, and they are free to release them through a process of divine healing. Divine healing is spiritual, and to receive immunity from the affects of sexual abuse, an infusion of a spiritual balm is essential.

Perpetrators of sexual abuse are controlled by a gross evil, one that is fueled to carry out its demonic deeds by way of a spirit that drives the perpetrator to do the unthinkable. It is inhumane to sexually violate a child or an adult. It is a violent, forcible assault that a person *in his or her right mind* cannot carry out. Accordingly, it requires a higher, more powerful spiritual power to overcome the havoc wreaked upon the human spirit by sexual abuse – a power that is not borne of humanism, contemporary thought, or psychological therapy, but is born of the Spirit of Almighty God. Just as anti-biotics are injected into the human body to ward off diseases, evil spirits are rendered powerless when the Spirit of God is infused into the human spirit. Good and evil cannot occupy the same space. Therefore, the refuse of evil (the haunting emotional and mental trauma) cannot remain to dominate the human spirit when God inhabits the soul, the mind, the will and emotions.

The miraculous deliverance that comes from faith in the power of God to eradicate the paralysis wrought by child sexual abuse are documented in volumes by those who, through the power of God, are finding healing and total deliverance. For those men and women, ready to be released from this bondage, it is *your* Time To Heal.

STATISTICS

Almost anyplace you go, you will find someone who has been sexually abused in his or her lifetime; the numbers are staggering. But for the purposes of this workbook, we will focus on childhood sexual abuse.

1 OUT OF EVERY 4 GIRLS IS ABUSED BY AGE 18
1 OUT OF EVERY 6 BOYS IS ABUSED BY AGE 18
MEDIAN AGE OF ABUSE: 9-YEARS-OLD[1]

KNOW THIS:
Abuse happens in your neighborhoods.
When you believe your children are not at risk, you will not pay close enough attention. They may pay a high price.

MORE STATISTICS

- 39,000,000 survivors (in the U.S.) are reported.
- Only 1 in 10 tell.
- 70 percent of all sexual assaults are perpetrated against children under age 17.

[1] http://www.cdc.gov/nccdphp/ace/prevalence.htm

PERPETRATORS

Who are the perpetrators?

90 percent of all abusers are acquaintances or family members, trusted and loved by their victims. Perpetrators take advantage of these relationships to exert power and control over their victims.

> That translates to only 10% of abusers as strangers.
>
> *Fathers* assault 1 out of every 5 children under the age of 12.

What does the Bible have to say?
And whoever welcomes a little child like this in my name welcomes me. But if anyone causes one of these little ones who believe in me to stumble, it would be better for him to have a large millstone hung around his neck and to be drowned in the depths of the sea.   Matthew 18:5-6

CONSEQUENCES

The consequences of child sexual abuse do not affect only the victims. Society is also victimized and pays the price. First, let's look at some of the consequences to an innocent victim.

In most cases, children do not understand why sexual advances are wrong; they only know that it doesn't "feel" right. They are not equipped with how to verbalize to an abuser to stop the action; they must be taught. And if they are not taught, they become easy targets for manipulation.

Children naturally respond to people who give them attention. They don't question the actions, because they are naturally trusting of those whom they know. Oftentimes, they even trust strangers if the attention feels good. Children want to generally please adults, so they are obedient, even in the face of confusion and impending fear.

When abuse occurs, a child is left feeling confused and scared about what happened, causing – in most cases – the child to go silent. Perhaps the perpetrator made threats (often about people the child loves) to the child if he or she "tells." The ensuing consequences cover a wide range of negative and destructive behaviors and emotions that overlap into the effects on loved ones *and* society in general. In many cases, a victim experiences more than one of these behaviors. Listed here are some of the most common and noticeable of those.

CONSEQUENCES

- Sense of shame, disgrace, torment, confusion, distrust
- Silence and isolation
- Self-mutilation and marginal existence
- Drug and/or alcohol dependence (70 to 80% of victims)
- Depression, post traumatic stress disorder (PTSD), anxiety, eating disorders (80 to 90% of victims)
- Suicidal thoughts or attempts (20 to 30% of victims)
- Difficulty forming long-term relationships
- Sexual promiscuity leading to teen pregnancy (60% of victims)
- Prostitution (greater than 90% of victims)
- Serial rapists (70 to 80% report themselves as previously abused)
- Serial molesters may have as many as 400 victims

LESSON 1 YOU ARE NOT ALONE

OPENING REFLECTIONS

Childhood sexual abuse is far more rampant than the average person can imagine, and the long-term effects upon a person's mind, will, and emotions are unimaginable – except to the victim. It is like tattered threads that weave unevenly through every relationship – jagged thoughts that serve to make us feel isolated. The silence we have swallowed for so many years empowers the fear we experience, conjuring feelings of shame and unworthiness, often making us feel undeserving to be well regarded, respected, or esteemed. Consequently, the well-buried secret of abuse that we carry, along with the threats of harm should we reveal this horrid secret, feeds our sense of isolation on a daily basis. This deception contributes to our isolation, even though we have learned to put on a happy face or use some other means, to mask our fear and sense of abandonment, while we struggle through every day. We yearn to cry out while we hold in our secret. But healing is possible with God.

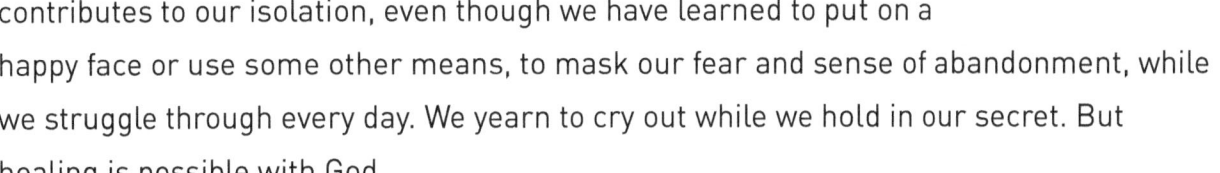

The real secret is that there are often people all around you who experience the same feelings of being alone. They are being different in a way that is hidden; they use the same defense mechanisms to shield their feelings of inferiority or isolation. From the section on statistics, spelling out the numbers of adult survivors of sexual abuse in America (39 million "reported" – not including those not reported), those numbers alone speak to the fact that surely you are not alone. As you embark on this journey of healing, you will be surprised at the profiles and personalities of those who share the same secret – a secret which must be expunged from your heart to allow healing to begin.

> Take a few minutes to describe some of the feelings (if any) of being alone or isolated because of what happened to you as a sexually abused child. _____
> _____
> _____
> _____
> _____

> How did those beliefs about being alone or isolated affect your relationships with others? _____
> _____
> _____
> _____
> _____

BUILDING THOUGHTS

When we feel alone or isolated, even though we may have learned to shield or cover our feelings from others, our thought life is fed with vulnerability and leaves us open to toxic, self-effacing untruths. The enemy of your soul is a master at convincing victims of sexual abuse that the crime was their fault, or that they somehow attracted the crime to themselves. The reason these thoughts have been such strongholds in your life, is because they are held captive by the silence you permit in order to protect the real enemy – the person(s) who brought harm to you, and the evil power that overtook that person to do the evil deed. **However, for every difficulty we face, there is always a solution, and the solution to abuse begins with a choice to be healed.** That choice comes with a determination that you will no longer guard the silence that has kept you a prisoner of your thoughts. As a man (or woman) thinketh, so is he or she.

We acknowledge that what was done to us was not our fault! We face THE TRUTH that the person or persons who harmed us were absolutely wrong. We face THE TRUTH that we will not be ruled by the thoughts that we are somehow responsible for what happened to us. We face THE TRUTH that we are not guilty, and there is no need for us to be ashamed. We were victims of a thief who – like one stealing valuables – stole our childhood. That thief (who may have been a family member(s), robbed us of our innocence. We must be willing to be transparent enough to face these issues that haunt us. When we face these un-truths head-on, we face THE TRUTH. **These are issues born of our thought life. They come from the lies Satan himself tells us:**

- ▶ LIES that make us believe we are not esteemed and valued by God Himself, or others, in our circle of influence.
- ▶ LIES that cause us to feel ashamed, when we are not the cause of the crime(s) carried out against us. We are survivors who were victimized.

The guilt remains with our perpetrator(s).
- ▶ LIES that make us feel sexual intimacy in marriage is degrading or not to be enjoyed without shame or guilt.
- ▶ LIES that we cannot achieve our dreams because of what has happened to us.
- ▶ LIES that we do not deserve loving relationships because we feel unworthy or damaged.

PROVOKING QUESTIONS

What lies do you have to reject that are not TRUTH about your life?

That: _____

That: _____

That: _____

That: _____

Others: _____

_____

Applying the Balm of Scripture

You shall know (recognize, realize, come to the knowledge of) the TRUTH and the TRUTH shall set you free. John 8:32

The Lord Jesus has promised: **I will never leave you or forsake you. – Hebrews 13:5**

This promise is quoted 366 times in scripture. Consider one for each day of the year – and even an extra one for leap year. You are NEVER alone, and confidence in that promise will free you to be confident around others. It will cause you to refute the lies that Satan's evil thoughts have whispered to you about yourself. **God has declared the devil a liar and the father of every lie. (John 8:44) His certain doom is clearly spelled out in scripture.**

God's Mercy (on our behalf) and TRUTH have met together; Righteousness and peace have kissed. TRUTH shall spring out of the earth, and righteousness shall look down from heaven (on your behalf). **Righteousness shall go before Him, and shall make His footsteps our pathway. – Psalm 85: 10-13**

Determine to walk in that path He has opened for you. Our Father, God, has said to us: **"I have no greater joy than to hear that My children walk in TRUTH. – (3rd John: 3)**

CLOSING REFLECTIONS ON LESSON

A quick study of statistics at the beginning of this workbook must assure you that you are not alone. Without realizing it, people empower their eroding secret of childhood sexual abuse by remaining silent. Perpetrators depend upon that silence to continue their crimes without being held accountable and to be protected from prosecution. Because this problem is everywhere, it is very possible that a co-worker, a family member, a close friend, or even the person sitting next to you in the pew has suffered silently with the very same pain of childhood sexual abuse that you have endured. How reassuring would it be for that person to know he or she is not alone?

Imagine a world where, finally, people open up about this epidemic, causing treatment to become widespread. Those who abuse will no longer have the refuge of your silence to protect them. Their threats are usually veiled or implied to assure the silence of their victims who fear these threats. Thankfully, adult survivors of childhood sexual abuse and increasing numbers of children are emerging from their silent closet sanctuaries to reveal the secrets that have held them captive – a step that will set them free. It is not  always an overnight freedom. In most cases, it is a process. However, it is a process whose time has come. Now is the time to break the silence.

LESSON II   THE POWER OF TWO: DON'T START THE PATH ALONE

OPENING REFLECTIONS

In the multitude of counselors, purposes are established. And two are better than one. Human beings – all life forms for that matter – are created with dependency upon others for sustenance. The human body has been designed marvelously and wondrously, having the capability to heal itself from many diseases and infections When the limitations of the body are, however, unable to ward off aggressive diseases or external trauma, help is required to sustain life. This is especially true when both the body and the spirit have been wounded with sexual abuse. The internal bleeding of the human spirit begs for the comfort and consolation of another trusted and nurturing human being. The challenge for such unhealed souls who have reached adulthood is to discover where to go for such solace.

What steps have you taken to seek a trusted friend, counselor or support group?

_____
_____
_____

BUILDING THOUGHTS

Today, there are many sources for adult survivors to find help. Because our research shows that true liberation from this emotional and mental trauma is found in faith-based programs, we strongly urge adult survivors to find a counselor or confidante you trust.

Look for a church sponsored support group for survivors of child sexual abuse. Even with the spiritual support available in church settings, it is important to not take comfort in becoming isolated in these support groups. To remain silent in a support group is to allow fear, anger, resentment, and resistance to fester, which only adds to the difficulty of finding healing for your soul. This is, in effect, defiance in the healing process; the enemy seeks these openings as a way to keep you imprisoned.

Don't start the path to healing alone. Submit yourself to trust the nurturing and compassion of those who have experienced similar circumstances in their childhood years and have discovered freedom from a life of torment. Your courage to trust a counselor or those in a support group can be the catalyst for someone else's healing, simply by finding hope and encouragement from your experience.

PROVOKING QUESTIONS

Have you encountered the unfortunate and insensitive comments of those who may know of your struggle and who offer harsh statements like: "Oh, just forget it! You have to move on with your life"? It is a common misunderstanding of the depth of the damage done to your psyche. How have you addressed this kind of response from those with whom you may have shared your secret?_____
_____
_____

What prompted your decision to ultimately seek help? _____

_____
_____
_____
_____

Applying the Balm of Scripture

Becoming familiar with scripture (the Word of God) will lead one to incredible insights for all experiences we face. Once we make that discovery, we yearn to know more about God's character. The Word is a healing balm, and we develop a divine dependency upon His love and care as we build a personal relationship with Him. Because He is your creator, He understands all that concerns you, and He promised that He **"would perfect that which concerns you." Psalm 138:8** As you consider reaching out to find consolation in a trusted counselor or church-affiliated support group, remember, it was the Word of God that said, **"Where there is no counsel, the people fall; but in the multitude of counselors, there is safety." Proverbs 11:14**

We have learned through dependence on the Word of God, and the trusting relationship that comes from growing in Him, that there is nothing we can encounter of any magnitude where there is not instruction and guidance, compassion and encouragement. Crowning verses sustain us in every circumstance as He gives us the following assurance in **Psalm 32: 8:** "I will instruct you and teach you in the way you should go; I will guide you with My eye," and **Jeremiah 29:11-13**: **"I know the plans (thoughts) I think toward you, says the Lord, thoughts of peace and not of evil, to give you a future and a hope. Then you will call upon Me, and I will listen to you. And you will seek Me and find Me, when you seek Me with all your heart."**

Finally, for the encouragement of His abused children, He adds: **"And all who prey upon you I will make a prey. For I will restore health to you and heal you of your wounds, says the Lord." Jeremiah 30:17**

CLOSING REFLECTIONS ON LESSON

We acknowledge that healing is your choice. We trust that you have come this far in your choice for healing because you recognize the need for the strength that can come from aligning yourself alongside a trusted counselor. You are encouraged to allow yourself the time you need to become involved in a small group setting of others who are also on the same path toward healing. There is power in numbers of those with like experiences to share, air the pain of the past and healing in the present. The dissembling of old mind control mechanisms occurs voice by voice, time by time, to render powerless those controls, which only operate by your permission. When you can disengage those controls in the company of trusted others, they are seen clearly for what they are: false fears – incapable of being controlling agents over your life.

LESSON III   IT IS TIME TO BREAK THE SILENCE

OPENING REFLECTIONS

We have all heard the saying "Silence is Golden." But life experiences have a way of twisting the integrity of a statement that was honorable and beautiful into something ugly. "Fractured Fairy Tales" comes to mind. These were supposedly comic twists on fairy tales to entertain kids, which were produced in animation for TV. Unfortunately, many kids grew up on the twisted version of the stories and never really knew the real, untainted version of these fairy tales. In much the same way, children who have been sexually abused are introduced in a violent, twisted, perverted way to what was designed to be a beautiful, intimate expression of love between married couples.

These initial assaults upon their innocence follow them into adulthood, often infringing negatively on practically every relationship they'll have. Their trust in people they love and care about is often threatened, because of their being violated at an early age by those they did once trust. **And because that trust has been violated, the children become convinced that they can trust that adult to carry out the threats to harm them and those they love, such as their moms, or another loved one, if they "tell."**

Children do what all frightened children will do, they retreat into silence. (The exceptions are if they have been taught not to withhold such information, or if they are naturally assertive or self-motivated.) It is a deafening silence – one that buries years of muffled, internal screams with pillows stained with tears. Angela's Voice is resolved to do just as its name declares: To give a voice today to those who choose to heal. Life is about choices – through the good times and through adversity, we all make choices.

- ▶ You can make the choice to heal-or not.
- ▶ You can make the choice to be diligent in understanding how your abuse has skewed your interpretations and responses to life's events.
- ▶ You can make the choice to learn healthy and balanced decision making.
- ▶ You can make the choice to learn new ways to view life's adversities.

If you have shared the experience of your childhood abuse, describe your feelings afterward: _____

_____
_____
_____
_____
_____
_____

Are there yet unresolved feelings that you believe must be addressed and that you can share? _____

_____
_____
_____
_____
_____
_____

**Are you willing to take a step toward breaking your silence? Yes ____ No ____
Please explain:** _____

_____
_____
_____
_____
_____
_____

BUILDING THOUGHTS

You are participating in this program because you have recognized the long-term damage that childhood sexual abuse has brought to your life. It is safe to assume you are weary of harboring the hidden pain and carrying the burden of weight that silence forces upon your soul. You are making a critical step toward ridding your life of the baggage your past abuse has heaped upon you, a liberating step toward removing the obstacles of your thought life. This will be important in bringing your thoughts into verbal expression, where they can be dealt with and eventually eradicated.

Breaking your silence is a choice. If you acknowledge the need to break your silence, write what you believe will be the personal benefits to your decision:

_____
_____
_____
_____
_____
_____
_____

PROVOKING QUESTION(S)

What are the personal risks you know you must take to break your silence?

_____
_____
_____
_____
_____
_____
_____
_____

You must want your freedom of mind strongly enough to risk whatever the consequences may be. How prepared are you emotionally and mentally to handle those consequences, knowing that to be healed, the risks must be taken? Explain how you are prepared or unprepared to take this step: _____
_____
_____
_____
_____

Applying the Balm of Scripture

To paraphrase the Bible, God works in mysterious ways, and His wonders are awesome to behold. This is a truth that applies not only to things God does in Creation and according to His divine character, it also applies to the things God does through us – His children. God is not the source of evil occurrences in our lives. He hates the evil deeds wrought against us, and His anger and judgment burn against our doomed enemy. But scripture assures us that God has a mysterious way of turning what Satan meant for evil into good. Often, those things seem strange, even unfair; but God always has a reason for turning circumstances around that will ultimately bring about His purpose IN us.

"Not only so, but we also rejoice in our suffering, because suffering produces perseverance; perseverance, character; and character, hope; and hope does not disappoint us, because God has poured out his love into our hearts by the Holy Spirit, whom he has given us." (Romans 5: 3-5)

Sometimes the perfection He works through us comes through suffering. It certainly happened with His only Son, Jesus, who endured unbelievable suffering, all for the purpose of paying the ransom heaven required, that sinful man could be restored to God. The cost of that ransom was the sacrifice of blood, shed from an unblemished, perfect Lamb. Jesus was that perfect Lamb. Without His suffering and death at Calvary, we would be forever doomed from Adam's original sin. **(Luke Chaps. 22-24)** Remember, scripture reminds us that **"Good people do not always escape troubles. They have them too. But the Lord helps them, each and every one." (Psalm 34:19 L.B)**

Applying the Balm of Scripture

In like manner, God turns the suffering we have endured into miraculous things. Consider this: automobiles may have been what **Proverbs 8:12** (KJV) refers to as "witty inventions" that God put into the mind of man as an alternative means of providing transportation, while sheltered from exposure to the harsh elements. Prior to its invention, hundreds of families suffered and died from cross-country pilgrimages in cloth-covered wagons through searing heat, snow, wind, sand, and rain storms. Similarly, God turns the suffering of childhood sexual abuse into a ministry like Angela's Voice. It was Angela's miraculous delivery by God that turned her suffering into an international ministry to bring healing to countless others. Many in turn, become prepared to reach out to those who will continue sharing Angela's message of healing and freedom.

CLOSING REFLECTIONS ON LESSON

Opening up your heart about the pain of your past is important to your well being – physically, emotionally, spiritually, and socially. When you commit to bringing expression to the pain of your struggle, the responses of others must not be a deterrent to your choice to be healed. You must want to be free for your own peace more than what others may think. This is an area where you must trust in Almighty God, who wants to see you delivered. **In fact, It is God alone who has put the desire in you to be set free of your past. He makes that clear in Philippians 2:13**, which declares that God is already at work within you, causing you to want to do His good will, and His good pleasure. That is such an awesome act of love. This offers a great opportunity to activate your faith and trust in your Creator.

LESSON IV   KEYS TO BREAKING THE SILENCE

OPENING REFLECTIONS

In chapter II, we discussed your readiness to make a significant choice to break the silence you may have lived with most of your life. We reflected on the loss of trust with those whom you trusted, and the impact such loss often has on your subsequent relationships. We considered the importance of placing your personal needs for freedom from the past far above any concern for what others might think. Your peace of mind is not dependent upon how others might respond to your choice to do what is best for you.

We have given you opportunities to express in writing your feelings about sharing your past and your willingness to face any mental or emotional risks that might result from your decisions. Your preparedness to handle consequences of breaking your silence was linked with just how determined you are to be free.

We considered the positive outcomes that can be derived from circumstances where we have overcome severe suffering. Finally, we revisited the scriptural example that illustrates the ultimate reward of sacrifice: God's only Son, Jesus, willingly endured the worst suffering and execution known to man which culminated at Calvary. But His death paid the cost of our access to an abiding relationship with God through His Son and paved the road to eternal salvation.

Now that the need to break the silence has been assessed, it is essential to determine just how to break that silence. There are specific keys to that process ... and it is a process, but one well worth the time and devotion required, not only to enter the door to deliverance, but to come through victoriously.

BUILDING THOUGHTS

When you have been victimized by a sexual predator, you are not the guilty party. As simplistic as that "sounds," the majority of men and women who were sexually abused as children have been made to feel ashamed, unworthy, powerless, hurt, incapable of loving relationships, and that the assault upon their bodies was somehow their own fault. Nothing could be further from the truth.

From today to as far back as Biblical times, families have shied away from any discussion about sex, even when it was simply to teach children about reproduction. To sidestep the issue, society commonly referred to (and continues to refer to) sex talk as 'the birds and the bees.' No one wanted to use the word "sex." In fact, when it was absolutely called for, it was often spelled out as S.E.X., implying that to even pronounce the word was to speak profanity. Indeed, for many years, the Federal Communications Commission (FCC) ruled that the word "sex" was not allowed to be uttered on radio or television. Early TV family-oriented sitcoms (now in syndication), such as The Dick Van Dyke Show, Ozzie & Harriet, and The Lucille Ball Show were only allowed to show twin beds in the married couple's bedroom. Today, the pendulum has swung with a loud bang against the wall on the other side of the spectrum. The FCC rules no longer apply.

The unfortunate fallout of this hush-hush, puritanical attitude over the generations has caused the violent crime of sexual abuse to also fall into a hush-hush domain. This rendered:

1) **the perpetrator to become empowered by the silence to continue his/her crimes; and**
2) **the child became a silent victim, often made to feel ashamed and guilty, as though they consented to the crime,**

exacerbated by the veiled threat that "they'd better not tell, or else harm would come to them or to their loved ones." Consequently, whether parents or others knew or did not know about the abuse, no one wanted to talk about it. This behavior is beginning to show signs of change as reflected by the many government and private agencies that have been developed to protect children and prosecute predators. But the ugly truth remains that 39 million reported adult survivors, and countless more, still need healing. These are the adults who were raised to live in silence about the violent crimes enacted against them. Healing is now available.

Fill in the blanks below to affirm your resolve against accusations or wrong thoughts about your childhood innocence:

It was never my fault when _____
_____

I renounce and reject every accusation against my innocence, and I declare that I was NOT _____
_____

I release my talents and gifts to flourish without the fear of anyone discovering past crimes of sexual abuse or violent sexual assaults against my child self; with that admission I am free to – _____
_____
_____
_____
_____

I agree now to RELEASE THE SECRET of the sexual assault against my innocence and my body: I release the hold of silence over my life and will not fear those who disagree with my decision. I know that to continue my silence is to empower the FEAR and TORMENT that controls me. I CHOOSE to open a dialogue in the safety of trusted confidantes and counselors and in support groups, along with other survivors who have made the decision to break the silence.

_____ I agree with the above statement:
_____ I choose peace and joy over pain and suffering
_____ I need more time to overcome the silence
_____ I choose to be brave in the face of family and friends' denial.
_____ I agree, it's time to break my silence
_____ I need more time

PROVOKING QUESTIONS

What relationships stand to improve with your decision to openly dialogue about your childhood victimization by sexual abuse? _____
_____
_____

Do you have faith that as you develop a trusting, personal relationship with God, your healing – through the love of Christ Jesus on your behalf – is assured?
_____
_____

Have you acknowledged the crucial role you play in your healing – that you must choose to practice the keys to break your silence? _____
_____
_____

Applying the Balm of Scripture

Scripture teaches us that Jesus suffered every abuse known to man. When it comes to the matter of sexual abuse, how would you describe the fact that He was publicly stripped naked, tied to a whipping post and beaten mercilessly with these whips? According to Roman custom, the whips consisted of several leather strips; each loaded with jagged pieces of metal and bone, and weighted with heavy lead. After being stripped naked of His clothes, which the soldiers gambled for, He was hung in that condition upon the Cross until He died. This biblical truth is clear, despite the sanitized drawings and film images of a battered, bloodied Savior being covered with a loin cloth on the Cross. We know that His death was violent – an abuse so painful that one cannot imagine it. **(Matthew 27:23-34)** To add insult to injury, He was mocked, spit upon, stared at, and ridiculed. **(Psalm 22: 13, 17)** This is shared to make it clear that Christ too has borne all of our sorrows and all of our grief; but that His abuse, suffering, and death were the price He paid that we might be purchased as His own. He took our sin upon Himself in order to restore our relationship with God the Father for all eternity.

CLOSING REFLECTIONS ON LESSON

Let's compare your healing to the life of a butterfly: a caterpillar is the beginning of a life cycle. It crawls along, mostly hidden in its environment. Sometimes it is ugly, and people shy away from it. When it is ready to morph into a flying insect, it builds a cocoon to insulate itself, while it changes into its final stage of life – a beautiful butterfly. **"Better is the end of a thing than the beginning thereof."**
Ecclesiastes 7:8

That caterpillar is like you. When you go through the stages of healing, beginning with the courage to stand up and 'commit to admit' what was done to you as a child, you will totally disarm the enemy of fear that has controlled you for so many years. Using the keys to break your silence, and leaning on your growing trust in God, you can transfer the power you have given your silence and overpower the false perception of its control over you. With the help of God, you are now in control. The cocoon of intimidation in which you have hidden for far too long will begin disintegrating. Soon you will be seen emerging as a beautiful monarch butterfly. You will take flight to a liberated life for the first time in the brightness of a renewed you. We will rejoice with you in your freedom!

LESSON V — THE PURGING POWER OF PRAYER

OPENING REFLECTIONS

One of the most endearing promises of God is: **"I will help you." Isaiah 41:10** Here is the consummate love of God the Father, reaching to His sons and daughters. It is an invitation to spend time with Him. In those few words, God is offering Himself to us, to be entreated for His love, compassion, and tender care. Essential to effective prayer is our faith in God. The best way to develop faith in God is to get to know Him.

As we get to know one another by spending time together, so it is with God. We spend time with Him in quiet meditation, reading His Word, and talking to Him. We do not need to speak in "thees, and thous" to talk to God. God knows your way of talking, and He accepts you as you are. Profane words He will not accept, because He has much to say about the use of profanity; He will never go against His own counsel. God has described Himself as our friend, our elder brother, our Father, and of course, our Savior. To know Him in all of those relationships is to know the love of God that passes all understanding.

To make a decision to get to know God, start with prayer. Talk to Him as a friend; find a special place, and plan to meet there with your Lord every day, preferably early, before your day starts. Get a good daily devotional as a companion to a good Study Bible. Starting with the Psalms will speak more to your emotions, or you may begin at the beginning with the Old Testament, or the New Testament. Wherever you choose to begin, pray for God to give you the wisdom to understand what you read. Simply make a commitment to God that you will strive to meet Him in prayer at that place each day. He cherishes your commitment; He will meet you where you are.

BUILDING THOUGHTS

Prayer is the most powerful and effective form of communication. It is simply talking with God. Does He answer? Yes, God answers. He can answer with either a yes, no, or not now. Sometimes God is silent, allowing our faith and patience in His all-knowing wisdom to grow; those times are not easy. Waiting is never easy when a parent says, "Not now," causing you to wait. There are numerous scriptures and stories in Bible about the rewards of waiting.
(See Isaiah 40:31)

But waiting has another benefit. It purges the dross of impatience, rebellion, wrong motives, and many other ungodly attributes that need cleansing from our spirits. This happens as we continue in prayer and are led by God's empowering Word. When His still, small voice convicts us of offensive thoughts, deeds, plans, and unworthy pastimes, we are moved to allow His love to prick our hearts. Soon we find our thoughts akin to His thoughts and our desires akin to His desires for us. That is the purging power of prayer.

Another powerful aspect of praying is called praying the scriptures or praying the Word of God. When you learn His promises, you can pray them back to God: "Lord, you said if I delight myself in You, you will give me the desires of my heart." That is praying the scripture. God delights to hear you pray His Word back to Him.

When it is necessary for an immediate answer, God knows how to perform mighty and miraculous acts on our behalf. There again, however, what God deems as necessary for an immediate answer is not always in keeping with our must-have-now schedules. For patience in the times of immediate needs, it is good to be a person with a consistent habit of prayer. When prayer becomes part of a daily lifestyle, when we plan for it, look forward to it, have faith in our prayers, and anticipate times alone with God, we confront life's "sudden lies" with a level-headedness that only comes from a close relationship with God. That intimacy through prayer with the Almighty prepares us to handle what otherwise might shake our very foundations. To be prepared is to be pre-prayed.

How does your life reflect your relationship with God? _____
_____
_____
_____
_____

Is there a void in your life that you feel prayer could fill? _____
_____
_____
_____
_____

Would you like to learn more about how to develop a prayer life and a relationship with God? Yes _____ No _____

How has prayer influenced your life? _____
_____
_____
_____
_____

PROVOKING QUESTIONS

Has the sexual abuse you experienced caused you to resist the thought of praying? _____
_____
_____
_____
_____
_____

Do your thoughts cause you to question where God was when you were being abused? _____
_____
_____

Would you like to have your questions about prayer and God's knowledge of your abuse answered? _____
_____
_____

Applying the Balm of Scripture

In the "Opening Reflections" portion of this, Lesson V, one phrase was quoted from the passage in **Isaiah 41:10**, but it is fitting here to quote the entire passage in verses **10-11 of Isaiah 41**. "Fear not, for I am with you: Be not dismayed, for I am your God. I will strengthen you. Yes, I will help you. I will uphold you with My righteous right hand. Behold, all those who were incensed against you shall be ashamed and disgraced. They shall be as nothing, and those who strive with you shall perish."

The Bible tells us that all of God's promises are yes and amen. ("Amen" meaning: It is so, most assuredly, so.) Having the faith to believe His promises gives us hope. The Bible also says that **"Hope does not make us ashamed."** Our lives become so incredibly empowered when we apply the Word of God to every situation. That is why praying people do not come apart at the earliest sign of trouble. They pray instead.

The Bible also acknowledges that we have a temporary enemy here on earth in the person of Satan; but scripture also arms us with the faith in knowing that Satan and his demons tremble when they see the weakest saints upon their knees in prayer, wielding the power of the name of Jesus as they speak to Almighty God. What is your heart cry? Ask. Charles Spurgeon, noted theologian, once said: "Whether we like it or not, asking is the rule of the kingdom."

"Ask and you shall receive." John 16:24 That simple utterance to God is praying. Believing you will receive, as indicated in **Matthew 1:22** and **Mark 11: 24**, is the simple step to faith God desires, that invites you to ask what you will of Him. As you pray, God will know the desire in your heart and He wants you to be conscious of your motives for what you ask. For when we pray, we must come before God with sincere hearts and pure motives, lest we ask amiss and not receive from God. **James 4:3** In your time of meditation, let these scriptures inspire your growth in faith.

CLOSING REFLECTIONS ON LESSON

Prayer has purging power. It is a cleansing agent for the soul. The fervent prayer may often be accompanied by repentant tears, joyful tears, and pleas for forgiveness of known and unknown offences toward God. Prayers touch the heart of God, and He moves on our behalf. This is affirmed in God's words, which declare that **"The effectual, fervent prayer of a righteous man avails much." James 5:16**

Whatever you need at the moment you need it, pray about it. Then seek to know God, for the answer is always found in Scripture – if we take the time to search for it. Whatever we're feeling, whatever we're suffering, whatever we're hoping, God has something to say about it in His Word. The Bible has been aptly called "The Owner's Manual." We belong to God. He created us; being our "man"-ufacturer means that he knows everything about us. How appropriate, then, for us to read the Owner's Manual when we need help trying to navigate through life. We need the fuel injection of the Holy Spirit to keep our hearts well tuned.

To desire God, to passionately search for Him, will never be a futile effort. His promise throughout the Bible is that, if we seek Him with all our hearts, He will be found by us. That begins with prayer and a desire to know Him. He says of His desire toward us that we **"might grope for Him and find Him, though He is NOT far from each one of us." Acts 17:27**

LESSON VI UNMASKING

OPENING REFLECTIONS

The title of this lesson is a lesson in one phrase: take off the mask. We offer these five guidelines in unmasking what sexual abuse has stolen from your true identity. If there was ever an identity theft, it was at the hands of a perpetrator of sexual abuse. Make these statements, speak these affirmations and resolve to take these actions often:

- ▶ I AM WHO GOD MADE ME TO BE, NOT THE FALSE IDENTITY MY PAIN HAS CAUSED.
- ▶ I CONFESS TO JESUS CHRIST, TO MYSELF, AND TO A TRUSTED ALLY, MY STRENGTHS, MY GOD-GIVEN GIFTS AND TALENTS, AND MY WEAKNESSES.

- I CONFRONT THE FALSE APPEARANCES OF MY TRUE SELF, AND TODAY, I BEGIN PEELING OFF THE LAYERS OF FALSE IDENTITY THAT MY PAIN AND TORMENT HAVE CAUSED. I AM WORTHY AND I ACCEPT THAT I AM MADE IN THE IMAGE OF GOD. I ACCEPT THAT GOD SEES ME WHOLE AND PURE, AND I SEE MY TRUE SELF EMERGING AS GOD SEES ME.
- I AM LEARNING TO EMBRACE AND LOVE MY TRUE SELF AS I SEE MYSELF EVOLVING LIKE A BUTTERFLY FROM A NO-LONGER-NEEDED COCOON.
- I DO NOT HESITATE TO CONTINUALLY SEEK THE WISDOM AND SUPPORT OF A PROFESSIONAL COUNSELOR.

Applying the Balm of Scripture

When God created mankind, He created us in His image. Ever since Satan was cast out of heaven and took a third of the angels with him (his demonic pawns), he has attempted to dis-figure the image of God within mankind. Scripture speaks against Satan and his futile attempts to mar the wonder of man's creation as stated in **II Corinthians 5:17**: "If any man be in Christ Jesus, he is a new creation. Old things are passed away. Behold (or look with awe), all things are become new."

Again, we are reminded that Satan is a thief who steals whatever he can from us. He will make us believe that we are less than the worthy men and women God has destined us to become. **John 10:10** says, "The thief does not come except to steal (your rightful identity), and to kill (your purpose), and to destroy. I have come that you may have life, and that you may have it more abundantly."

CLOSING REFLECTIONS ON LESSON VI

VALUE YOURSELF: RECITE THESE TRUTHS ABOUT YOURSELF:

- I AM VALUABLE
- I AM BEAUTIFUL
- I AM BLESSED
- I AM SMART
- I AM BRAVE
- I AM THE APPLE OF GOD'S EYE: PSALM 17:8
- I AM TRUSTWORTHY
- I AM FEARFULLY AND WONDERFULLY MADE: PSALM 139
- I AM MORE THAN A CONQUEROR: ROMANS 8:37
- I CAN DO ALL THINGS THROUGH CHRIST: PHILIPPIANS 4:13

LESSON VII BREAK OLD HABITS AND SELF-DESTRUCTIVE PATTERNS

OPENING REFLECTIONS

'Think outside the box' is one of today's most over-used clichés. But that cliché is a perfect description when considering the boxes we survivors of sexual abuse use for escape. These boxes are safe havens for the wounded children hovering in our souls. As adults, those boxes become prison cells, and the patterns with which we learned to survive inside those boxes, from childhood to adulthood, cramp our vision to move unrestricted by fear or poor self image. Sometimes it even short circuits our ability to move with confidence into our destinies when great opportunities present themselves, even though we are qualified and prepared.

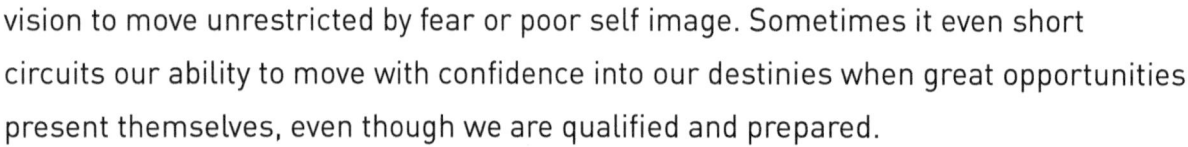

The net effect of the fear, the feelings of not being good enough, or the worries about what others think about us, have a way of creating defense mechanisms to validate the negative thoughts of not deserving better. Those defense mechanisms form "survival patterns" of behavior that have the potential to be self deceptive.

1) **You learn to survive by hiding your old patterns from others.**
   This is similar to "Masking," which we covered in Lesson VI.
   Yet, on the other hand,
2) **You may not be aware that others can sense your feelings of unworthiness and your poor self image. Remember, no one will see your beauty or your worth until you do.**

So you find yourself making excuses -
- ▶ For not applying for that position when you know you are qualified.
- ▶ For avoiding the interested glances of an attractive, would-be suitor.
- ▶ For not committing to intimate relationships with friends, family, or others.
- ▶ For declining a leadership role that others believe you can fill.
- ▶ For justifying lifestyles you know are damaging to your health or well being.
- ▶ For hateful attitudes toward people who remind you of your perpetrator(s).
- ▶ For procrastinating.

Pause for a minute. Name some patterns or habits that have linked themselves, to your disadvantage, as an adult: _____
_____
_____

When you have identified some of the patterns that have held you back from your potential—such as procrastination, worry over what others think of you, placing blame on others for your lack of responsibility, hostility toward others, sexual promiscuity, uncontrolled anger, dependency on uncontrolled substances, whatever you can honestly admit is a pattern that has negatively impacted your thinking, your behavior, and your life success, do this:

***For the next 21 days, begin and end your day by standing in front of a mirror and verbally denounce those traits. Declare that they are imposters and that they will no longer have residence in or rule your life. Behavioral research has proven that what we do (consecutively) for 21 days can easily be adapted into habit-forming results.

When you see evidence of the negative traits returning, get back on the 21-day track. At the end of each morning and evening's self-declaration before a mirror, end with the God-backed scripture: **"I can do all things through Christ which strengtheneth me." Philippians 4:13** The "eth" on the end of that word means *continually*. Post affirmations around your house to read often, such as: "I am the expression of unlimited potential in a world of infinite possibilities." Also, post scriptural affirmations such as the one above from **Philippians 4:13** and other promises from God.

BUILDING THOUGHTS

The literary world and, more specifically, the Bible, are filled with life-changing prescriptions for ridding one's self of debilitating and destructive life patterns that serve only to dismantle God's plan for your life. Go to any bookstore, and the most visible book shelves are those that contain hundreds of how-to books for changing your life. That there are thousands of such books written every few years is certainly telling about how we live. Publishers can't get enough of them, because people are always looking for ways to improve their lives. Most of these books are simply re-writes of the same formulas, but with new twists or slants. Most are contemporary rewrites of scripture; that is a proven fact.

Concepts of belief systems such as the attractor factor, positive thinking, and a plethora of other books, tapes, CDs and DVDs, are 90% Biblically based. The difference is, when you add Christ and your faith in His all-powerful force to the equation, the challenge to change is not as hard,

because He goes before you as your advocate. More than you, He wants to see you victorious over your bad habits and patterns. Admittedly, old habits don't die without a fist-fight; but you enter the ring already a declared winner when you take Christ into the fight with you. One famous boxer said as much of his phenomenal wins.

When it comes to making a quality decision to break the patterns that are ruining your life, yes, it will be a fight. But you'll get there when you are armed with greater faith and trust in the only one true lover of your soul. God promises us a safe landing, but not always a calm passage. Ask Jonah. What an example! Adversity is the training ground for faith. As we have said throughout this workbook, however, the choice to change belongs to you. Make a choice to break old patterns. Study Jonah's plight in the Book of Jonah.

PROVOKING QUESTIONS

How dedicated are you to break the patterns that have served only to deter your dreams? _____
_____
_____
_____

Do you believe that Christ has your best interests at heart and that He longs to help you live your best life? _____
_____
_____
_____

What, if any, doubts do you have or drawbacks do you see to your potential to break old habits?
_____
_____
_____
_____

Applying the Balm of Scripture

There are thousands of verses of scripture to assure us that no matter what we need to change in our lives, God being for us is more than the whole world against us. God knew before any of us were born that there would be adversities we'd have to face. But in His infinite love and wisdom, He has promised to be with us in every battle we have to face, no matter what enemy we face, even if that enemy is in-a-me (as someone penned it humorously); but even with those strongholds within us, if we allow Christ to be within us, He will lead us valiantly and victoriously to conquer all our foes.

Here is an all-inclusive promise available for you and all those who love Christ. It is an awesome assurance that nothing has the power to overtake you when you are in Christ Jesus. Let it absorb deeply into your conscious decision to allow God to help you break every stronghold.

Make the conscious decision to allow God to help you break every stronghold that withholds you from your dreams. Excerpts from this promise are found in **Romans 8:31-39**: **"What then shall we say to these things? If God is for us, who can be against us? He who did not spare His own Son, but delivered Him up for us all, how shall He not, with Him also freely give us all things? Who shall bring a charge against God's elect? It is God who justifies ... Who shall separate us from the love of Christ? Shall tribulation, or distress, or persecution, or famine, or nakedness, or sword? ... Yet in all these things, we are more than conquerors through Him who loved us. For I am persuaded that neither death, nor life, nor angels, nor principalities, nor powers, nor things present nor things to come, ... nor any other created thing, shall be able to separate us from the love of God, which is in Christ Jesus, our Lord."**

CLOSING REFLECTIONS ON LESSON

Has all this reference to scripture, to God, and to God's love for you not sat well with you? Don't fret, and certainly don't allow your resistance to these Godly things to throw you off the track toward your principal goal of finding healing from the trauma of the abuse you suffered. Many of us have been where you are; many of us resisted; many came to the end of the rope – angry and fed up with the demons that haunted us at every turn.

We too have struggled with imposters in our dreams, our decisions, our relationships and our hope to one day be free of the anxieties that keep us paralyzed. Don't give up the goal to be free. We are here for you. If you are not open to the faith-based proven methods we ascribe to at Angela's Voice, we will listen to you, and still walk with you toward healing. We care for all who come to this ministry for deliverance, even those who cannot understand or are not ready to accept God's intervention in their life. First and foremost, we want to see you set free. Enjoy your victories, large or small, and don't beat yourself up for the failures.

LESSON VIII FACING FOE(S) BY CONFRONTING IN LOVE

OPENING REFLECTIONS

You have broken your silence. You have made the choice to face the inner strongholds that have affected your relationships and decision-making. You have recognized that you are not alone and that there are trusted counselors and others who are on the same path to healing who are available to support you. You are also learning to value yourself and to acknowledge the gifts and talents that you have been given. You are open to breaking old patterns that are the result of your childhood sexual abuse that caused you to escape to the safety of an imprisoned, emotional lifestyle. You are moving out of that box to openly face the world and those around you.

It is time to face those (whether living or deceased) who harmed you.

There are conditions for confronting your perpetrators, those living and those who have passed this life. Those conditions will determine how you go about confronting their crimes. You're almost there in your healing. You want to be confident that this is the right way, the only way, to lay to rest your struggle with your past. Understand that you are about to totally disarm your enemy. You have finally come to recognize that the only control your perpetrator still has over you remains embodied in your silence and your refusal to expose the crime that was committed against you.

Let's begin by acknowledging the power you released to yourself by breaking your silence in the company of a trusted counselor and others who are engaged in this process. This was the beginning of melting the tip of the iceberg. As the waters of other hidden emotional barriers begin to recede around you, the demons that haunted you are gradually exposed. The iceberg of sexual abuse will begin to emerge as the visible foe it was. You have acknowledged, as these emotional barriers begin revealing themselves, that you are NOT the guilty party, nor are you responsible, nor are you unworthy. The enemy of your innocence has now emerged in full view for you and others to see . Now it is time to face that foe. But there is a certain path you must take – you are almost there.

This is the moment when you will use the wisdom of a professional for guidance. You are not to concern or weigh down yourself with the "whys" of your abuser's actions against you; you may never know what prompted this person to commit the wrong done against you. That is a burden that must be borne by the perpetrator alone. You are on this journey for your own deliverance, not the perpetrator's.

Your abuser must face his or her crime independent of your healing. Here is the path you must follow: You must approach your perpetrator empty of accusations. You both already know what was done. In order to avoid the anger and contempt that would compromise any attempt to make this important step negligible, or one that would backfire, you must submit to a purging process to rid yourself of the venom of resentment and unforgiveness that is poisoning your life. Without purging all residue of hatred, contempt, or any subconscious desire for vindictiveness or revenge, you will compromise your nearly complete path toward healing.

BUILDING THOUGHTS

The path toward healing will prepare your heart to approach those who harmed you as a child. This demands a willingness to acknowledge your motives. It is essential for complete deliverance that, before you confront those who have caused your pain, that your motive is for you and you alone. It is to fulfill your need to release the silence their threats have held over you for so many years. The act of describing the act of rape, or incest, or forcible acts upon your innocence, to the person who violated you will completely disarm and dismantle the secret they have trusted you to keep. That single act alone dethrones the threats, the fear, and the control that the secret has held over you. That is the whole purpose of the confrontation – to free yourself of that false threat and power that has held you captive for so very long. That, and that alone must be your single motive for confronting your perpetrator. That leaves no room for hostility or viewing the time of confrontation as an opportunity for revenge – to "strike out" with a motive to "strike back."

You must approach your abuser with a steady, controlled voice and an even temperament, yet with positive confidence in this necessary confrontation. A confrontation that empowers you to say to your abuser that you will no longer be silent about what was done to you (saying exactly what it was they did), and assuring them that you will be open to sharing or exposing what was done to you as a child to every one else that needs to be informed, without fear of any consequence or reaction from anyone.

You will speak with bold assurance that you are ready to be released from the secret that has kept you imprisoned for __ years, and that with this open acknowledgement or confession of the wrong that was done to you, you are once and for all free to be whole. **Never confront your abuser alone. Always take a trusted friend or family member with you.**

PROVOKING QUESTIONS

Before we take the final step toward your healing, you must confront your own readiness to release any hostility, anger, vindictiveness, or need to exact pain on your perpetrator(s). Use this space to express any unreadiness you have for releasing your need to strike back. I am not ready to release my hostility against my perpetrators because: _____
_____
_____
_____
_____

I am willing to do what is necessary to prepare myself to approach my perpetrators, free of hostility. I want freedom from the emotional trauma of my childhood abuse badly enough to: _____
_____
_____
_____
_____

Applying the Balm of Scripture

Here are reassuring words to comfort you as you consider the need to have a clean heart and a renewed, right spirit to approach your perpetrator(s). For every wrongful deed that was done to you, remember, God has instructed us clearly: **Vengeance is mine, saith the Lord, I will repay. (Romans 12:19)** We cannot play God or bring correction to those who have trespassed upon our lives. That is God's work. Allow this Psalm to undergird your resolve to let God be God in the matter of your need to release the hostility you may harbor. This excerpt from **Psalm 37** assures you that God can take care of your enemies, and give you His peace. However, even as God judges wrong doers, He still allows them an opportunity to repent and be forgiven, if they come sincerely before Him, confessing their wrongs against you. For those who have passed this life, their judgment is with God.

"Do not fret because of evildoers, nor be envious of the workers of iniquity. For they shall soon be cut down like the grass, and wither as the green herb. Trust in the Lord and do good … feed on His faithfulness … Commit your way to the Lord, Trust also in Him, and He shall bring it to pass. He shall bring forth your righteousness as the light and your justice as the noonday … Do not fret because of him who prospers in his way, because of the man who brings wicked schemes to pass. Cease from anger, and forsake wrath … it only causes harm. But the meek shall inherit the earth, and shall delight themselves in the abundance of peace."

CLOSING REFLECTIONS ON LESSON VIII

Confront those who have caused you pain whenever possible, except when it would result in physical, mental, emotional, or spiritual harm to yourself or others. Face them in a spirit of forgiveness and accept that they may not be accountable or admit their guilt for their actions. However, you must be responsible for your own actions, not theirs. This is especially true when you feel a need to be vindictive, or when you want to strike out at your perpetrator, as you confront them. This would make futile your efforts to be delivered from the power of the secret. Why? Because it would instigate a new onslaught of resentment and hostility to the already paralyzing and traumatic life of emotional distress from which you are striving to be healed. The answer is to confront in love, not condemnation. **(Again, this should be undertaken with the guidance and wisdom of a professional counselor.)** Be ready and willing to surrender to God. We encourage you to become an active member of a church home. Learn to receive love. Let go of the anger and let go of the shame in order to embrace the love of God.

So, now how exactly do you confront a person who sexually violated you as an innocent child? That's the next step: The final answer to your healing.

LESSON IX FORGIVENESS: THE FINAL ANSWER TO TRUE HEALING

OPENING REFLECTIONS

Forgiveness is an act that carries miraculous properties. Something divine happens within the heart of the person who does the forgiving and something divine also happens within the heart of the person who truly accepts one's entreaty for forgiveness, so they may be relieved of their offence. The aspect of the divine nature of forgiveness is due to the fact that true forgiveness is an act of God. Man's will to forgive another for the burden of their offence moves the heart of God, and God performs the surgical removal of the offence and causes the heart of the receiver to accept. It is a supernatural attribute of God toward man.

Whether the predator or perpetrator accepts your forgiveness is not tied to your decision to forgive them for what they did. When you forgive with your heart, you are divinely released. You are no longer held captive by the stronghold of unforgiveness within yourself. Unforgiveness has been linked scripturally and scientifically to numerous

diseases – from dryness of the bones to all types of cancers. It has something to do with speaking things from one's lips that reflect the issues of the heart, which is directly linked to those things coming into being. That is why the whole phenomenon of "positive thinking" has changed people's lives. It is directly related to a power that has been given to man to speak things into being.

Accordingly, when one speaks sincere words of forgiveness to another, he or she moves into a place of miraculous freedom. It is a divine work, and is not contingent upon lip service only, but it is directly related to sincere words of forgiveness spoken from the heart. We have been empowered through what we speak, to speak life or death to our situations. (**Proverbs 18:20-21**) It is a gift from The Creator, who "spoke" all things into existence. It is the Genesis story.

Words have power. The old adage: "Sticks and stones may break my bones, but words will never hurt me" is one of the greatest misconceptions children hear in the playground. It is spouted as a defense against the one who has verbally berated them. Consider the child who has been told he or she will grow into greatness. When that child sincerely believes that, it will happen, regardless of circumstances. The same holds true for the child who is told he or she will never amount to anything. If that child believes that, he or she will be a failure, unless intervention occurs to circumvent that wrong thinking. Again, it is true, "as a man thinketh, so is he." It follows, then, that forgiveness, spoken from a heart that has been readied to forgive by releasing hostility, anger, revenge and a desire to strike back at the perpetrator, is a heart that can speak words of true forgiveness. When that occurs, that man or woman receives the divinely imputed power to overcome and be released from fear, doubts, feelings of inferiority, feelings of isolation, powerlessness and the demons that deliver all of those "false thoughts and feelings." They will walk with a new walk, with a new confidence and leave behind the chains that fall powerless behind them. All caused by the divine agency of forgiveness.

BUILDING THOUGHTS

Forgiveness is treating those who have hurt us with the same full compassion and love that we wish to be treated – by those WE have hurt. Forgiveness is treating those who have hurt us with the same full compassion and love that we wish to be treated – by those we have hurt. That statement bears repeating. Why? Because we have all hurt someone. And hurting people tend to hurt others. Therefore, the above statement bears repeating. It is a precursor to our need to forgive those who have hurt us.

Forgiveness is:

- ▶ Accomplished in the Power of Jesus Christ. Man does not have that power.
- ▶ Man's willingness to surrender his will, to allow God to empower him to forgive an offender. Man cannot, of himself, forgive. God honors man's desire to forgive.
- ▶ Must be genuine
- ▶ Is an act of obedience
- ▶ Is liberating
- ▶ Is a prayerful petition
- ▶ Is completely selfless
- ▶ Is absolutely essential
- ▶ Surrendering vengeance to God's hand
- ▶ Continual: Matthew 18:22
- ▶ Highest level of spiritual maturity

Forgiveness does not release your abuser from accountability.

PROBING QUESTIONS

Forgiveness requires a total commitment on your part. Are you ready to forgive?
Yes _____ No _____ Explain how and why you have come to your decision:
_____
_____

Check the areas where there may be residue of the following in your heart:

Anger _____ Resentment _____ Jealously _____

Vengeance _____ Hatred _____ Others _____

Would you like to speak to a counselor about helping you rid yourself of those areas? Yes _____ No _____

Feel free to express any comments on your responses here: _____
_____
_____
_____

Applying the Balm of Scripture

Forgiveness is the very foundation of all God's purposes in His relationship with mankind. From the very beginning, God made a blood sacrifice for forgiveness in the Garden of Eden, after Adam and Eve sinned. Their first move was to attempt to cover their sin from God.

It is human nature for us to try to cover our sin. Offer a child an "either or" choice of cookies. They can have the peanut butter, but not the chocolate. That is for later. One they may have, the other they are not to touch. Which one are they most likely to choose? Let Mom walk in the kitchen while their hand is holding the chocolate cookie, and at her appearance, the guilty hand immediately goes behind their back. Reading personal email at the office, the employee clicks to the work screen seeing the boss approach. If caught, they need forgiveness or face unhappy consequences.

Applying the Balm of Scripture

Covering (or attempting to cover) our faults is human. That's why Adam and Eve "completely covered" themselves with fig leaves to hide from God after disobeying Him about which tree not to eat from. The pictures you see of a naked Adam and Eve with a fig leaf each are not scripturally correct; they were completely covered, resembling bushes. God was grieved over man's sin; so in order to acceptably cover that sin, killed an animal in the garden (blood was shed) and took the skin of that animal to "cover" their nakedness of the glory that was lost. That was why they felt naked. The glory of God had left them when sin entered. And they felt exposed. Now here's the beauty of God's forgiving love:

"Covering by blood" is God's way of redeeming us back to Himself, or paying heaven's required ransom to restore fallen mankind to Himself, which Satan attempted to steal from God by tempting Adam and Eve. So a blood sacrifice was required to cover the first man and woman's sin. Man has absolutely no power to forgive without God. That's why forgiveness is a divine work that is wrought when man surrenders His will and desire to forgive, to God.

So the first blood sacrifice to cover man's sin was not at the Cross of Christ; what God did in the Garden was a fore-shadowing of what He would ultimately do, eons later at the Cross. His sacrificial blood (through Jesus) is the ultimate agency for cleansing, forgiveness and redemption. All of this was done to bring forgiveness to man, from Adam to you and me. This is why forgiveness can ONLY be wrought by God Himself. How blessed we are, that His love and His shed blood, has paid the price for our sin. All we must do is accept what Jesus did for us, repent for our sins and receive His awesome forgiveness that has eternal benefits.

Applying the Balm of Scripture

Therefore, we must go to God for forgiveness for ourselves and to forgive those who hurt us

"To the Lord our God belong Mercy and Forgiveness." **Dan 9:9**

"Therefore, put on tender mercies ... bearing one another, and forgiving one another, if anyone has a complaint against another; even as Christ forgave you, so you must do." **Colossians 3:12-13**

"... If you have anything against anyone, forgive him that your Father in heaven may also forgive you your trespasses. But if you do not forgive, neither will your Father in heaven forgive your trespasses." **Mark 11:25-26**

"Jesus said, Father, forgive them, for they do not know what they are doing." **Luke 23:34**

"If we confess our sins, He is faithful and just to forgive us our sins and to cleanse us from all unrighteousness." **I John 1:9**

CLOSING REFLECTIONS ON LESSON

Forgiving from your heart is genuine and freeing. Anger and hate cannot co-exist with peace and love. Forgiveness is non-negotiable because God requires forgiveness. It is an act of obedience, not a feeling. Forgiveness breaks the destructive spiritual bond between people and it releases both sides into freedom and answered prayer. Read **Mark 11:23-26**

Finally: Forgiveness is the Final Answer to True Healing.

LESSON X OUTREACH & SUPPORT: THE HEALING THAT KEEPS ON HEALING

OPENING REFLECTIONS

You have come this far by faith. It has been a journey that you have determined was one that you were committed to take. Your experiences along the way to your healing have undoubtedly challenged your beliefs about yourself, and about others. And you may have made some surprising discoveries about how the details of your life experiences have been seriously impacted by the sexual abuse you experienced as a child.

As you reflect on the exercises in the workbook, the dialogue shared with your counselors and others in supportive settings, you might recall observing how a renewed sense of personal development began emerging in your awareness. A development that you became conscious was an emerging person, one beginning to feel the baggage of the past dropping off little by little.

Eventually, as you progressed through this program, you may have experienced a resistance to completely emerge outside of a cocoon that, while it was miserable, it had become familiar, and so you may remember retreating to the comfort of the discomfort you have been accustomed to for so many years. But emerge you finally did. You broke your silence; you faced your old patterns and began breaking through them to embrace right thinking. You managed or are still working to manage the confrontations of those who violated you. And you sought prayer to petition a purging of your heart and soul to be readied for the ultimate freeing agency of forgiveness.

As you walk away to a restored sense of well being, look back to those who will come behind you. They will begin the path that you have taken and come through – bloodied, perhaps, but unbowed. As you reflect on those who will come behind you, consider how taking their hand might be a source of encouragement to them, as were those who stood alongside you in your journey. The need for your coming alongside those is welcomed and the need is great.

You may encounter someone along the road (whether in the workplace, a neighbor, a friend, or someone next to you in the pew), who may be suffering in silence as you have for so many years. It is now safe for you to be conversational about the road you have just taken. Such conversations can serve to open a crack in the door of someone's silence, so that you can help to open a door to their healing.

You now have a testimony that can help someone else heal. There is no testimony without a test. And you have the added benefit of continuing the healing process as you administer a bandage to someone else's wound, because you've been there and done that. It is what we like to call: The Healing that Keeps On Healing.

BUILDING THOUGHTS

Be willing to share your testimony. Many will be overcome by the words of your testimony, and you will be personally rewarded as you see yourself becoming a mentor to those who are beginning a process you have come through. You can inspire them of the freedom that will come with sharing the secrets they've kept. You can convince them by your experience that sharing their secret diminishes its power over their lives, and dashes the demons that accompany the secret to haunt their thoughts, dreams and life purposes. We urge and welcome you to:

- Share your spiritual awakening and healing process with others.
- Join or participate in a support group for survivors of child sexual abuse.
- Participate in a small Bible study group, and invite others to participate. It can be a positive help in influencing others, and continuing your healing experience.
- Take the step on behalf of others; that may take you out of your comfort zone, but will be a welcome invitation to others who need your support, and will edify you in the process.

PROVOKING QUESTIONS

Can you imagine yourself in a support group as an encourager to others beginning the process? Yes _____ No _____ What would cause you to decline?
_____
_____
_____

If you were convinced that by virtue of your participation in a support group, your life and the lives of others could be changed, would you be more amenable?

_____
_____
_____

Applying the Balm of Scripture

We have all been wounded. The great benefit, indeed the joy of taking the journey to healing with Angela's Voice has been nurturing as well as healing that has come from those who came and sat beside us, encouraging us, applying the balm of their counsel and care to our deep-seated emotional and physical wounds.

Many of us have felt just as the man known in scripture only as "a certain man." That could have been any man or woman involved in this program. Why? Because he was violently abused and abandoned. He had been on his way to a certain city, (from Jerusalem to Jericho), and on his way, encountered a band

of thieves who stripped him of his clothing, beat him unmercifully and left him for dead. Many times, we felt equally abandoned in our years of silence. But while this man lay severely beaten, naked and bleeding, a priest came down the same road, saw the man, and avoided him by going to the other side of the road. By and by, another man passed that way, looked at the abused man and retreated likewise, without reaching to help this victim of abuse.

How many among you have known those who knew you were being violated, and did nothing? That's why we need people such as you who've been wounded, to reach out to those still bleeding, who know people are passing by without helping, either because they don't see the wounds, or because they don't want to acknowledge the abuse or get involved like these two men?

Applying the Balm of Scripture

Finally, a certain Samaritan, on this same journey, came to where the wounded man was (as many have come as good Samaritans to our program). And when he saw him, he had compassion. And compassion is a verb. It moves people to act, not look and walk away. Then the Samaritan poured ointments on his wounds, bandaged them, set the man on his donkey, and carried him to an inn and took care of him. (That is what we do, and what we ask you to join us in doing for wounded men and women who come to this ministry).

As it turns out, the Samaritan was qualified to attend to those who were wounded, and went so far as to make certain when he was required by his business to leave the inn, to arrange for the innkeepers to take care of him until he returned, and did so by giving financial support to insure his care until he returned. The story is found in **Luke 10:30-37**.

We want to be fully prepared to help a large and growing group of people, who rarely have blood on the outside, but have incredible scars inside. Part of helping is to understand the symptoms and signals

We are looking for a few Good Samaritans to be an encourager, and a supportive mentor for those who have been wounded on their journey from childhood to adulthood by sexual abuse.

The Samaritan was not only there and willing to help, he was educated in how to bind the wounds, assess that the man would need longer-term help, and provide that help. What usually gets missed in this story is that he was educated enough to help.

LESSON XI CELEBRATING THE VITALITY OF VICTORY

Celebrating the Joy of Victory

What Does Victory Look Like to You?

- Victory Gives Me Passion For Life
- Victory Enables Me To Love Deeply
- It Frees Me To Develop A Strong Mind and Body
- I Am Liberated to Enjoy Dancing In The Rain If I Choose
- I Have Learned To Laugh At Myself!

(Things that used to embarrass me about myself now amuse me. I laugh alone and with others without concern about any thoughts others have about my renewed joy for life.)

- **I Can Now Risk Trusting Without Fear, Having A Renewed Sense of Perception**
- **I Am Freed To Enjoy The Benefits of True Intimacy**

SUMMARY

It is our prayer that the lessons contained in this workbook have served as a compass to guide you safely and faithfully through the other side of your healing process. Choosing, as you have, to deal with the trauma, we hope it has brought you to a place of understanding just how your experience with childhood sexual abuse damaged your body, your emotions, your thinking, your relationships and your spirit. Now that you have clearly seen your real enemy, and have confronted that foe, albeit with love and forgiveness, you are now freely enabled to securely walk through the door from your abuse to your healing. We celebrate your deliverance. We thank God for showing you, through His Word, the love He always had for you, and how He grieved over you as you were innocently harmed. We acknowledge His divine power that ushered you into His purpose, as you put your trust in His ability to impart the forgiveness necessary to restore you to Himself. We trust your becoming empowered will motivate you to share with others the hope that has been given you, through Christ Jesus.

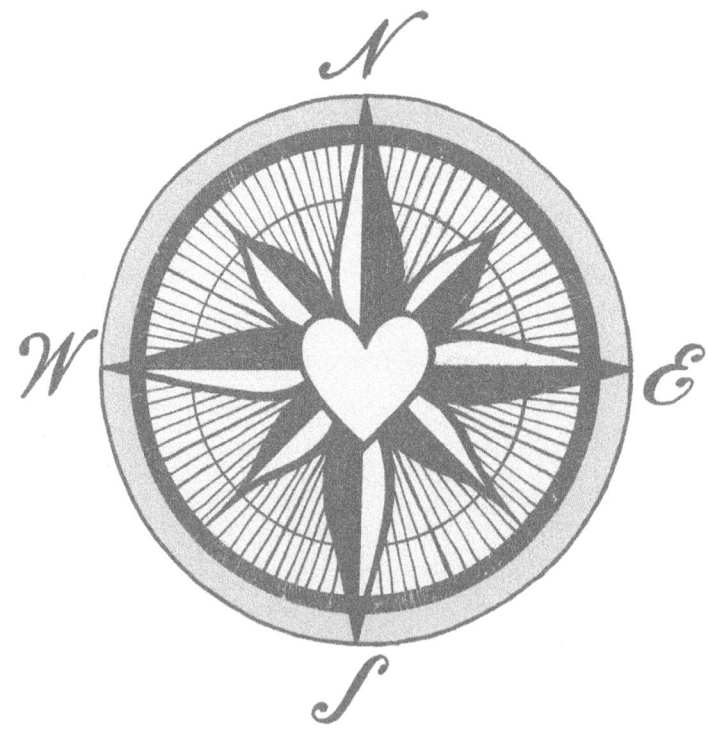

Angela's Voice

Angela's Voice is dedicated to developing, distributing, and endorsing valuable resources in the awareness, prevention, and healing of child sexual abuse. The materials, though specific for survivors of child sexual abuse, also benefit any abuse survivor and help protect children by teaching them how to defend themselves from abusive behavior. Founder Angela Williams, MFP, is a survivor-turned-advocate who shares a powerful message of triumph over tragedy by sharing her vulnerable and candid voice about her abuse trauma, her pain, her struggles, and her journey to healing in hopes that it may help other survivors expedite their healing journey.

Williams has devoted years to providing awareness, prevention, and healing programs through her advocacy work. Williams has captivated audiences with her powerful message of triumph over tragedy as a victim of childhood physical and sexual abuse. At age seventeen, she attempted suicide, and that day was the end of her torment and the beginning of a journey to healing. She is a crusader for change and dedicates her life to eradicate child sexual abuse. She holds a master's in forensic psychology with a concentration in child abuse. Williams is a powerful messenger, appearing in national and international news and documentaries. She has been successful in state legislative reform and national policy work and served on the Policy Committee of the National Coalition to Prevent Child Sexual Abuse and Exploitation. She has received numerous accolades and awards for her work, including her collection of books that have valuable lessons for survivors of all ages.

Please follow Angela Williams on social media and contact angelasvoice.com to book a speaking event or interview.

Books by Angela Williams

Loving Me: After Abuse
From Sorrows to Sapphires, Angela Williams's Memoir

Interactive Workbooks—Adults

<u>Healing</u>
Pathway to Healing, Guide to Healing
True Intimacy
Shattering the Shame
Unveiling Child Sexual Abuse

<u>Prevention</u>
Tough Talk to Tender Hearts
The Grooming Mystery
Single Parenting Solutions
Courage to Speak

Children's Books (Ages 5–10)
Gracie Finds Her Voice
Grant Gets His Shield
Gracie and Grant's Big Win
Gracie and Grant's Big Win Coloring Book
Find Your Voice Curriculum Book

Join the Angela's Voice Movement

Take action to break the silence and cycle of Child Sexual Abuse and Exploitation

HELP US SAVE THE NEXT GENERATION OF CHILDREN!

1. Be a Child Advocate
2. Donate at angelasvoice.com
3. Invite Angela Williams to Speak
4. Purchase another Angela's Voice Prevention or Healing Book

Discover more child sexual abuse prevention and healing resources at **angelasvoice.com** and follow angelasvoice in social media.

Instagram @Angelasvoice

Facebook @Angelasvoice

Twitter @Angelasvoice

Linkedin/angelasvoice

Angelasvoice.blogspot.com

Youtube.com/angelakwilliams

www.ingramcontent.com/pod-product-compliance
Lightning Source LLC
Chambersburg PA
CBHW040010080526
44586CB00028B/2950